Proverbial Adventures

Proverbial Adventures

Discovering Wisdom Alongside King Solomon

Angela R. Morris

RESOURCE *Publications* · Eugene, Oregon

PROVERBIAL ADVENTURES
Discovering Wisdom Alongside King Solomon

Resource Publications
An Imprint of Wipf and Stock Publishers
199 W. 8th Ave., Suite 3
Eugene, OR 97401

www.wipfandstock.com

PAPERBACK ISBN: 979-8-3852-2354-1
HARDCOVER ISBN: 979-8-3852-2355-8
EBOOK ISBN: 979-8-3852-2356-5
VERSION NUMBER 12/13/24

I humbly dedicate Proverbial Adventures: Discovering Wisdom alongside King Solomon to my beloved son, Aemilius.

As you continue to grow, my heartfelt prayer is that you encounter the triumphs that arise from embracing the wisdom found within the pages of Proverbs.

Son, please know that I hold an immeasurable love for you, and I encourage you to approach life one step at a time, knowing that your mother stands proudly by your side. Keep up the excellent work!

Contents

1

Introduction

So before blessing ourselves with the wisdom of God, we should first become friends with the word "proverb."

So what does a proverb mean?

Proverbs are like a treasure chest full of wise sayings and advice. It is like having a really smart grandparent who gives you lots of helpful tips for life!

Just like how you might ask your grandparent for advice on how to make friends or how to be kind, proverbs have lots of wise words to help you.

A good example of proverbs would be: "Kind words are like honey, sweet to the soul and healthy for the body." This proverb means that when you speak kindly to others, it only makes them feel good, but it's also good for your own health!

So, my children! Think of proverbs as a guidebook for life. It helps us learn how to be our best selves and make good choices. And there cannot be a better guidebook than the one written with the help of God himself—the Book of Proverbs!

The book of Proverbs is treasured with wisdom. I know you are probably asking yourself or your mother, "What exactly is Wisdom?"

I say you worry not and don't puzzle your wonderful mums; I will clear all your confusion.

The word wisdom is derived from 'wise,' which means to have knowledge, experience, and good judgment. So how does one know that they are wise? It is simple! You are wise because you are reading this book. You are able to read the words written in this book, which means you have knowledge and experience. You picked out this book from the book fair; this shows that have good judgment. So, I say you pat yourself on your back or maybe ask your mother to do that for you!

Wisdom means thinking wisely. So how can one think wisely? The answer is simple once again; you think wise when you read wise sayings!

The book you are holding in your hands right now is a book of wise sayings. The words wise and wisdom are found many times in the Holy Bible. Unfortunately, many people for whom the Bible was brought to earth do not understand what a wise person is.

For the men who wrote the Bible, wisdom meant much more than just knowing facts. The school you go to teaches you facts and lessons about maths, science, history, literature, and geography, but knowing the facts does not make a person wise. You may know a lot of things about animals, planets, or plants, but you may still not get along well with other kids. To be wise means, you know something about God and what He looks like. To be wise also means to apply what you know about God in your daily life. For example, God says in the Bible that the tongue has the power of life and death. If you are a wise kid reading this saying, you will automatically start to use your tongue for a good cause. You will speak in a manner that you won't hurt any person, you will shower your siblings with compliments, and you will greet your neighbors gently. To be wise means you understand God, and your understanding leads you to obey God as you should.

So now, with the understanding of wisdom, your curious little minds must be asking, "What is the Book of Proverbs?"

Here's the answer; the Book of Proverbs was written by men who knew a lot about God from their own experience as well as the experience of other people. Those incredible men understood that God is a loving father who wishes the best for his children. They understood that there are principles to live by if we wish to live a life of dignity. The men who wrote the Book of Proverbs believed that things that seem important to us, such as having money, being famous, and having a lot of friends, are not equally important as understanding God and allowing him to steer our lives. In their opinion, a successful life was living as if God were watching all our actions. If you live believing that God watches all your actions, then there is a good chance that you will not do wrong.

My children, you must know that God watches us for our own good. He watches over us so he can protect us all the time. We should not carry the belief that God is constantly monitoring us but instead take comfort in the idea that He will protect us from harm.

God himself is the source of wisdom. In the Old Testament, many kings and leaders sought wisdom so they could govern their communities better. King Solomon was one such king, and he was known to be wise. Like countless other men who were loyal to God and were famous for their wisdom, King Solomon was quick to understand that God gives us the ability to see the world and ourselves as we truly are. God has given us the brain, which is an organ that is powerful enough to invent other things. One of the amazing things about humans is that we can create incredible machines that can travel on land, in the air, and under the sea. Cars, airplanes, and submarines are some examples of these amazing machines that have changed the world and made our lives easier. We could not have invented these machines without the gift of intelligence that God gave us. He wanted us to use our brains to explore and discover his creation.

But the real wisdom is not inventing things because in inventing things, we are simply showing off the capability of our brain—something that was meant to be used. Real wisdom is the real understanding of how we are to live our lives, and it is something that only comes to people who love God.

4

People who love God know that he loves us so much, and he wants us to be happy and healthy. That's why he teaches us how to get along with our friends and family, how to be kind and not selfish, and how to think before we act so, we don't regret anything later. He gives us wisdom so we can live our best lives.

We, as children of God, should not be too concerned if we are not the most intelligent among our friends. God says that we don't have to be a brilliant person to be wise. The only thing we need to have is the right attitude and the understanding that God controls all of the universe. Once you have the right attitude and faith in God, you are definitely on your way to becoming wise. When you live in the love of God and act toward your friends and family with kindness, you are closer to being wise. When you read books such as the Book of Proverbs or Proverbs for Kids, your wisdom grows ever further.

Now, my kids, it is time that we learn the story of King Solomon. . .

WHO WAS SOLOMON?

A big big portion of the Book of Proverbs was written and compiled by King Solomon. Solomon was the son of King David, who ruled Israel a long while ago. Solomon had a reputation for being a wise man. The first instance of Solomon's wisdom was shown to the world when he was asked to judge in a famous case in the early stages of his reign as a king. There were two women who claimed to be the mother of the same child. The two women and the baby was brought before Solomon, who ordered his men to cut the baby in half. Solomon ordered that both women shall receive one half of the baby. Solomon's wisdom was brought to public attention when one of the woman asked for the baby to be given to the other woman. Solomon knew that the real mother would never make peace with her baby withstanding such cruelty. Solomon gave the new born to the compassionate woman, and his judgment was considered wise by his people. The historic judgment made the people of Israel realize that their ruler was intelligent and a great connoisseur (ask your mother to translate this) of human nature. The story of Solomon's judgment in the case of two mothers is mentioned in the Bible (1 Kings 3:16–28.)

Solomon could never be wise if he didn't seek help from God. When he became the king of Israel, he asked God to give him the wisdom to govern his people. Solomon had asked for wisdom when he could have asked for wealth, power, or for his enemies to be destroyed. He could have followed the path of the kings that ruled before him, but he valued wisdom more than anything materialistic. So God gave Solomon much more than he asked for. God was impressed, so he gave Solomon riches and fame besides wisdom.

Over in Egypt and Arabia, Egyptian and ancient kings were compiling collections of their own wise sayings. The Egyptian kings were especially well known for their knowledge of human affairs. However, Solomon surpassed them in his collection of wise sayings. According to his story in 1 Kings, Solomon is believed to have spoken more than three thousand proverbs. Many of those proverbs are preserved in the Book of Proverbs. Besides his contribution to the Book of Proverbs, Solomon also sang the song of Solomon and wrote the Book of Ecclesiastes. People from around the world would come to visit Solomon so they could hear his wisdom. He was wise about most aspects of life. He was not only familiar with human life; he was well informed and taught about plant and animal life.

The kingdom of Israel prospered under the rule of Solomon. In fact, Israel was larger than it had ever been during Solomon's reign. He was a wise ruler, and his enemies were afraid of him and his wisdom. They did not dare to attack Israel because they knew they would lose. Solomon constructed a magnificent temple in Israel. It was furnished in gold and bronze, and it was beautiful from the inside as well as from the outside.

The life of Solomon is a great example of most things taught in the Book of Proverbs: the ones who seek wisdom from God are not turned away without extra blessings.

The story of Solomon has a sad ending. In his last years as the king, he did not act wisely. Solomon was a king who had a lot of wives. Some of them followed different gods and convinced him to do the same. God didn't like that at all and decided to break up his kingdom into two parts. Solomon ruled for 40 years, and then he died. He was extremely smart and left behind some worthy advice for us to learn from. No one else in Israel was as wise as him. We're lucky we can read his words today.

2

Wisdom

Proverbs 22:17

> Incline your ear, and hear the words of the wise, and apply your heart to my knowledge,—Proverbs 22:17 (English Standard Version)

Proverbs 2:3

> Call out for insight, and cry aloud for understanding.—Proverbs 2:3 (Common English Bible)

Proverbs 19:8

> Do yourself a favor and love wisdom. Learn all you can, then watch your life flourish and prosper!—Proverbs 19:8 (The Passion Translation).

EXPLANATION

Proverb 22:17 encourages us to gather knowledge from the wise and apply their teachings to our lives. The wise are more experienced than us in all aspects of life. So we should listen carefully to their advice and apply it to the area that needs it the most.

As with many children, I think you could be someone who finds trouble sleeping. You could be thinking that there are monsters under your bed that keep you up all night and prevent you from getting a night of good quality sleep. The wise, if asked about your situation, would say, "The monsters and ghosts are only the creation of the mind. There nothing of such sorts exist."

Then, they would say and advise, "If you find trouble in sleeping, then you must have an empty mind. The empty mind is the house of the devil, so you must take up a hobby that fills your mind and makes you tired enough to sleep. Reading books and stretching is a good exercise to drain the mind and prepare you for sleep."

Proverb 2:3 encourages us to seek our wisdom and understanding from God. The proverb invites us to call out for insight and cry aloud for understanding and to search for it, as wisdom is a hidden treasure. Our intent to seek wisdom should not be less than seeking a hidden treasure because wisdom is no less than any treasure of this world.

When we cry out for understanding, we acknowledge the fear of the Lord and find the knowledge of God. Therefore, in doing so, we are steered into living the good Christian life, and as we grow up, we are presented as the ultimate archetype of humans.

Proverbs 19:8 emphasizes the importance of gaining wisdom and understanding. God in the Book of Proverbs, written and compiled by Solomon, promises that those who acquire wisdom and understanding will be rewarded with a better life.

This proverb claims that if we acquire wisdom, our lives will prosper and flourish. But how will our lives prosper? If we seek wisdom, we can gain a better understanding of how to make good choices, which can lead to an improvement in the quality of our lives.

The proverb also reminds us of the importance of having faith in God. We, as the children of God, must put our complete faith in him. In exchange for our faith, God assures us wisdom and understanding that we could use to live a life of purpose and meaning.

VERSES TO REVIEW

Proverbs 8:36

"But he who sins against me injures himself; All those who hate me love death."—Proverbs 8:36 (New American Standard Bible)

Proverbs 1:7

How, then, does a man gain the essence of wisdom? We cross the threshold of true knowledge when we live in complete awe and adoration of God. Stubborn know-it-alls will never stop to do this, for they scorn true wisdom and knowledge.—Proverbs 1:7 (The Passion Translation)

Proverbs 3:7

Do not be wise in your own eyes; Fear the Lord [with reverent awe and obedience] and turn [entirely] away from evil.—Proverbs 3:7 (Amplified Bible)

Proverbs 4:5–6

So make wisdom your quest—search for the revelation of life's meaning. Don't let what I say go in one ear and out the other. Stick with wisdom, and she will stick to you, protecting you throughout your days. She will rescue all those who passionately listen to her voice.—Proverbs 4:5–6 (The Passion Translation)

EXPLANATION AND TAKE-HOME POINTS

The Proverb 8:36 has a serious explanation. It warns us about the consequences of sinning against wisdom. The proverb makes a strong comparison between wisdom and death by saying that those who sin against wisdom are injuring themselves, and those who hate wisdom are taking themselves closer to death.

Although this comparison looks frightening, the verse is extremely valuable. We shouldn't be scared of whatever is written in the Bible because it is for our own betterment. Similarly, we shouldn't be afraid of death either; the only thing that should scare us is the wrath of God. Sinning against wisdom is like sinning against God.

Lying, dishonesty, and theft are some of the characteristics of those who aren't wise. Therefore, we should maintain distance from people who have these qualities and don't practice these traits even for a prank. The people who choose to sin against wisdom are actually challenging God. By committing crimes and collecting sins, they are injuring themselves and reaching one step closer to death.

Proverb 1:7 emphasizes the importance of having a healthy respect for God as the foundation of acquiring knowledge and wisdom. The proverb contains an interesting phrase that goes like this, "Cross the threshold of true knowledge." The interpretation of this phrase could be the existence of a point of entry. The proverb suggests that there is a point of entry or starting point for acquiring wisdom. The knowledge of interpreters and collectors of religious texts believe that the starting point mentioned in this proverb is indeed the obedient devotion to God.

"Stubborn know-it-alls" represents those who reject this starting point of wisdom. This phrase of the proverb serves as a reminder that those who have a sense of arrogance and pride and those who think that they know everything will never embrace true wisdom and knowledge because they are not willing to submit to God.

Proverb 3:7 calls us to rely on God. This proverb discourages us from relying on ourselves and wisdom and provides us with a better alternative. It asks us to rely on God and to turn away from evil.

However, to rely on God and absorb his wisdom, one must have approval from God. To get that approval, we should trust God completely for the reason that it leads to good judgment, common sense, and wisdom. We flourish like a tree when we put our trust in God, as our lives are filled with prosperity, happiness, and safety. Unfortunately, people who trust in themselves and are sure of their own wisdom are egocentric—a negative human trait and something despised by the Lord himself.

Aside from trusting ourselves, we shouldn't trust our money since it is simply a piece of paper that can never protect us from harm or evil. Also, trusting other men for answers is another dangerous trap. Trusting other men is like trusting a single thread over a piece of cloth or fabric to cover your whole body. Remember, disaster strikes like a cyclone, and the wicked are whirled away, but those who trust God have a strong character.

Proverb 4:5–6 again emphasizes the importance of gaining wisdom and understanding. A man is nothing but a fool if he trusts himself. Only a Simpleton believes whatever he is told, whereas a wise and sensible person will always check for God's word for wisdom and clarity.

The phrase "Stick with Wisdom, and she will stick with you" tells us that gaining wisdom will not be easy. We will be met with many burdens in our journey to gain wisdom. So we must stick by wisdom and undertake efforts to achieve it because the rewards are worth pursuing. It would rescue us from trying times and push us to our limits until we reach the hey-days.

The underlying meaning of this proverb suggests that obtaining wisdom may require sacrificing other things. In the later part of this proverb, Solomon even suggests selling all we have to obtain wisdom, indicating that it is that valuable.

The passage also emphasizes the importance of good judgment and insight. Acquiring good judgment and insight is just as important as obtaining wisdom and understanding.

Overall, the Proverbs explained in this chapter urge us to prioritize the pursuit of wisdom and understanding, even if it means sacrificing other things, to put our trust in God and seek his guidance regarding our lives.

3

Wisdom Part 2

VERSES TO REVIEW

Proverbs 4:7

> Wisdom is the most important thing; so get wisdom. If it costs everything you have, get understanding. (New Century Version)

Proverbs 3:13–14

> Those who find true wisdom obtain the tools for understanding, the proper way to live, for they will have a fountain of blessing pouring into their lives. To gain the riches of wisdom is far greater than gaining the wealth of the world. As wisdom increases, a great treasure is imparted, greater than many bars of refined gold.—(The Passion Translation)

Proverbs 2:6

> For the Lord gives wisdom; from his mouth come knowledge and understanding.—(English Standard Version).

EXPLANATION

Proverb 4:7 is the continuation of God's sayings that reflect his ongoing preference for wisdom. It once again conveys that wisdom should be anyone's top priority. Wisdom should be a person's top priority; therefore, we should seek it out and employ all our efforts in obtaining it.

The first part of the proverb states that "Wisdom is the most important thing," this means that wisdom is the principal of all things. As the followers of our Lord Jesus Christ, we must lay emphasis on wisdom as it would infect the decisions we make in life. Without wisdom, a person's decision and choices will reflect poorly as they find it difficult to navigate through the ups and downs of life.

The second part of proverb advises people to "Get understanding even if it cost everything they have." The deeper meaning of this verse translates into welcoming sacrifice in exchange of wisdom. The proverb suggests that wisdom is not something that can be easily obtained; it requires effort and sacrifice.

I sure you young minds will amount to something bigger and significant when you grow up. I am aware that you all will learn new concepts as you pass the middle school and transfer to high school, but at this point, I am also aware of the fact that many of you may not be able grasp the complete understanding of wisdom. Let me tell you that it is all right. You will understand wisdom better when you grow up. So for now, just remember that wisdom is not a concept that should only be tough in school, churches, or books; it is something that should be put into practical use. When you strive towards applying wisdom to your everyday use, your ability to make wise judgments will improve.

Overall, the NCV version of Proverbs 4:7 emphasizes the importance of wisdom, and encourages readers to actively pursue it as a means of developing good judgment and common sense.

Proverbs 3:13–14 is another collection of beautiful thoughts God has bestowed upon us through the book of proverbs (The Persian Translation). The distinguished verses provides us a revelation that those who find true wisdom not only gain an understanding of the world around them but also acquire the tools to live a purposeful and fulfilling life.

The phrase "fountain of blessing pouring into their lives," eloquently describes the benefits of true wisdom. This passage implies that wisdom gives rise to blessings and abundance in a person's life, such as peace, joy, and contentment.

The second part of the passage is the direct comparison between wealth and wisdom as it states, "To gain the riches of wisdom is far greater than gaining the wealth of the world. As wisdom increases, a great treasure is imparted, greater than many bars of refined gold." In the second element of the verse, God makes a claim that riches of wisdom will always be superior to the wealth of the world. , emphasizing the superiority of wisdom over material possessions. This suggests that while wealth may provide temporary pleasure, true wisdom provides long-lasting benefits and is far more valuable than any earthly treasure. Accepting the Lord's words with all heart, a loyal follower will not only consider wisdom superior than wealth, they would also defect from seeking validation in material possessions. While it is true that wealth can bring temporary enjoyment, true wisdom provides long-lasting benefits and is far more valuable than any earthly treasure.

Overall, Proverbs 3:13–14 in The Passion Translation once again commits to bring us closer to wisdom. It also encourages us to seek blessings (wisdom) and fulfillment beyond material possessions.

The Proverb 2:6 highlights the source of wisdom, knowledge, and understanding, which is the entity that exists above the skies. The complete passage of the proverb explains that true wisdom and understanding come from God because he is the ultimate source of knowledge.

By dividing this verse into two parts, we would get two different components. The first one states that "The Lord gives wisdom," implying that wisdom is a gift from God. The meaning of Lord giving wisdom is that humans cannot acquire wisdom solely through their own efforts, but must rely and depend on God to receive it.

The second component of the verse says that "from his mouth come knowledge and understanding," indicating that God communicates knowledge and understanding to humans through His words. Therefore, it could be said that reading the Holy Bible and studying scripture is a means of gaining wisdom and understanding.

To conclude, Proverb 2:6 in the English Standard Version reminds us followers that wisdom exists in the words of Lord, which means that true knowledge and understanding can only come from Him. If we want to develop an understanding of the world around us, we must study his words transcribed in the Holy Bible and in the other Gospels.

VERSES TO REVIEW

Proverbs 30:24–28

There are four things on earth that are small but unusually wise:

- Ants—they aren't strong, but they store up food all summer.
- Hyraxes—they aren't powerful, but they make their homes among the rocks.
- Locusts—they have no king, but they march in formation.
- Lizards—they are easy to catch, but they are found even in kings' palaces.—Proverbs 30:24–28 (New Living Translation)

EXPLANATION AND TAKE HOME POINTS

Proverbs 30:24–28 in the New Living Translation mentions four small creatures and describes the lessons that could be learned from them. The passage of the verse cleverly uses animals, mainly small insects and mammals as examples to teach us human beings valuable lessons about wisdom, commitment, resilience, and adaptability.

The first creature mentioned is the ant. Ant is praised in the passage for its wisdom to store food for the winter. In terms of structure, ants are probably the weakest insects in the world, but their preparation and foresight allow them to survive the harshest of weathers. Their preparedness teaches us the importance of planning ahead and being wise with whatever we have.

The passage then mention hyrax, a small mammal, who is praised for its ability to make its home among the rocks, despite not being strong enough. The example of hyrax is given in the passage to teach us about the resilience and the importance of adopting to our environment. Like hyrax, we too should utilize our strengths and surrounding and thrive under circumstances that may not suit us.

Locus is another insect mentioned in the proverbial passage. It is commonly known as grasshopper and is renowned for migrating long distances in destructive swarms. The locust, without a king, is able to march in formation with others of its kind. The tiny insects teaches us valuable lessons in life—we should place great importance in community and work together towards a common goal. We shouldn't shy away from seeking each other's support since great things are achieved people work together.

In the last few lines of the passage, the ability of lizard is praised. It is pointed out that lizards, despite being fragile and easier to catch adapt and thrive even in the most unexpected places, such as in King's palaces. A King can buy himself all the luxuries of this world but can't keep lizards out of his home. This teaches us about flexibility and adaptability, and the importance of being able to adjust to changing circumstances.

4

Pride

There is a wise saying that says, "Pride comes before a fall." The meaning of this saying is when we become too proud or full of ourselves, we often end up making mistakes or getting into trouble. That is why pride is mostly discussed in a negative light in the Old Testament as well as the Book of Proverb. The Old Testament describes pride as 'Self-centered attitude of superiority or arrogance.' If we take it upon ourselves to review Christian literature, we will know that the Book of Proverbs in the Bible has a lot to say about pride and why it's important to be humble.

Now I know words like 'Self-centered' could be overwhelming for your young minds, so let's first get to know and talk about what pride is. Pride is feeling like you are better than other people. It is a feeling or the state of mind that makes you think you are smarter, stronger, or more important than everyone else. Let it be known that there is nothing wrong in believing you are strong or smart, however, you must maintain humility at all times and never think better of yourself compared to others. Sometimes, when we're proud, we might even be mean to other people or make fun of them. That's not a very nice thing to do! For that exact reason, The Book of Proverb has specified pride as a negative human trait because it encourages selfish behavior and also suggests that those who have pride lack humility before God.

The Book of Proverbs says that being proud is something that God despise, which means that it is a sin! That might sound scary, but all it means is that it's something that God doesn't want us to do. Instead, God wants us to be humble and a helping hand to those who are disadvantaged. Humility means that we don't think we're better than anyone else. We're just happy to be who we are and to be loved by God.

The act of pride is considered a sin and on the topic of sin, The Book says,

"If anyone respects and fears God, he will hate evil. For wisdom hates pride, arrogance, corruption, and deceit of every kind. Ignoring sins lead to sorrow; speaking out against sins lead to peace. To do right honors God. Blessings chase the righteous! To sin is to despise God. Sin brings disgrace, and the wicked are crushed beneath their load of sins. Curses chase sinners. Who can say, "I have cleansed my heart; I am sinless?" Sin is atoned for by mercy and truth; evil is avoided by respect for God.—Proverbs 8:13/ 10:10,16/ 11:5/ 13:21,22/ 14:2,32,34/ 16:6/ 17:19/ 18:3/ 19:28/ 20:9

So, why does God link pride with sin or something bad? Well, for one thing, pride can lead to arguments and fights. When we think we're better than someone else, we tend to start an argument with them to try and prove that we're right. But that's not very kind, and it doesn't solve anything.

Pride can also lead us to make mistakes. When we're too proud to admit that we don't know something or that we made a mistake, we keep on taking the wrong path instead of asking for help. In taking those routes, we develop the wrong attitude which only makes things worse! That is why God encourages us to admit when we don't know something or when we've made a mistake. He also encourages us to seek help from him and also our elders. That way, we can learn from our mistakes and do better next time.

Pride is discouraged in Christianity and goes against Christian principles because it causes us to become unhappy. We become unhappy because we're always thinking about ourselves and how great we are. We usually forget to be grateful for the good things we have in our lives. Over the passage of time, we slowly begin to detach from people that care about us and we lessen the values of things that we once considered worthy. But when we're humble, we can appreciate the people and things around us that make us happy.

So, what can we do to be humble instead of proud? One thing we can do is to be kind to others. When we're kind, we're not thinking about ourselves and how great we are. Instead, we are self-less as we constantly think about the less privileged and we use our energy toward making plans and provisioning ideas about helping them. We can also be grateful for the good things in our lives. Humility gives us the feeling of gratefulness, and believe me when I say gratefulness is the greatest feeling, because when we're grateful, we're not thinking about what we don't have, instead we appreciating what we do have.

So, before we get to explaining the proverbs in this chapter, remember—being proud might seem like a good thing, but it can actually cause a lot of problems. So always try to be humble, kind, and grateful. That way, we can be happy and make the people around us happy too!

VERSES TO REVIEW

Proverbs 16:18

> Your boast becomes a prophecy of a future failure. The higher you lift up yourself in pride, the harder you'll fall in disgrace.—Proverbs 16:18 (The Passion Translation)

Proverbs 11:2

When you act with presumption, convinced that you're right, don't be surprised if you fall flat on your face! But walking in humility helps you to make wise decisions.—Proverbs 11:2 (The Passion Translation)

Proverbs 13:10

Pride leads to conflict; those who take advice are wise.—Proverbs 13:10 (New Living Translation)

Proverbs 16:5

Exalting yourself is disgusting to the Lord, for pride attracts his punishment- and you can count on that!—Proverbs 16:5 (The Passion Translation)

Proverbs 16:19

It is better to be of a lowly spirit with the poor than to divide the spoil with the proud.—Proverbs 16:19 (English Standard Version)

Proverbs 18:12

Pride comes before a disaster, but humility comes before respect.—Proverbs 18:12 (Common English Bible)

Proverbs 21:4

Haughty eyes, a proud heart, and evil actions are all sin.—Proverbs 21:4 (New Living Translation)

Proverbs 21:24

An arrogant man is inflated with pride—nothing but a snooty scoffer in love with his own opinion. "Mr. Mocker" is his name!—Proverbs 21:24 (The Passion Translation)

Proverbs 26:12

Do you see a man who is wise in his own eyes? There is more hope for a fool than for him.—Proverbs 26:12 (English Standard Version)

Proverbs 27:2

Let another praise you, and not your own mouth; a stranger, and not your own lips.—Proverbs 27:2 (English Standard Version)

Proverbs 29:23

One's pride will bring him low, but he who is lowly in spirit will obtain honor.—Proverbs 29:23 (English Standard Version)

EXPLANATION

Proverb 16:18 warns us that pride comes before a fall. In other words, when we become too proud or think too highly of ourselves, we are more likely to make mistakes or experience failure. This proverb encourages us to be humble and recognize that we are not perfect. When we are humble, we are more open to learning from our mistakes and seeking help when we need it.

The latter passage of the verse, "The higher you lift up yourself in pride, the harder you'll fall in disgrace," expresses the brilliance of our creator. It tells us that he is the most just. The passage explains that the disgrace (or humiliation) would be equal (almost identical) to our pride, meaning that the more we think of ourself today, the more isolated and forgotten we will become one day.

Proverb 11:2 teaches us that pride and humility have different outcomes. Those who are prideful of their wealth or physical features or boastful of their class may ultimately suffer shame and disgrace, while those who are humble and modest are most likely to find wisdom, grace, and honor. This proverb encourages us to be humble instead of arrogant, opening us to the probability that we might not be right all the time. It gives us a new perspective that others may have more valuable insights and perspectives compared to us. Lastly, this verse tells us we can save ourselves from the out-turn of pride and develop a feeling of appreciation by simply being humble. "But walking in humility helps you to make wise decisions," need I say more?

Proverb 16:19 in the English Standard Version states, "It is better to be of a lowly spirit with the poor than to divide the spoil with the proud." This verse again sheds light on the importance of humility and makes us knowledgeable about the dangers of pride. Through the medium of this verse, God tells us that it is better for a man to be humble and live contented with an ordinary life than to be proud and seek wealth and power at the expense of others.

In this verse, God also highlights the significance of maintaining relations with those who are less fortunate. Staying in the company of the poor helps to keep us grounded. Being around the poor helps to keep us humble and reminds us to be grateful for the resources and connections we have. In contrast, being around the proud and powerful can lead us to become prideful ourselves and to lose sight of what is truly important in life. When we are in the company of the proud and powerful, we are self-motivated to emulate their lifestyle, and in doing so, we upset God unintendedly and sometimes intentionally.

Altogether, Proverb 16:19 encourages us to cultivate a spirit of humility and to value relationships over material wealth and power. By doing so, we can live more fulfilling and meaningful lives.

Proverb 21:24 discusses the connection between pride and wickedness. The verse then suggests that pride is a root cause of all sins. The verse also reminds mankind and the followers of Jesus Christ of the negative outcome of pride. When we allow ourselves to become arrogant and prideful, we distance ourselves from God and from others. We may become selfish and tend to disregard the feelings and needs of those around us. This self-concerning mindset and dishonorable lifestyle soon leads to a life of sin and misery, both for ourselves and for those we interact with. Overall, the verse in Proverb calls us to be mindful of our attitudes and to guard against the dangers of pride. If we strive to learn humility and prioritize serving others, we can avoid the pitfalls of sin and experience a blissful life.

Proverbs 27:2 primes mankind about the dangers of self-promotion. "Let another praise you, and not your own mouth; a stranger, and not your own lips," means that it is better to receive praise from others than to praise ourselves. We should not act in a manner to draw attention towards ourselves or accomplishments. People love attention nowadays; they use various channels such as, social media, news, and other platform, to bring the focus onto themselves. While it could be a great feeling, knowing that you are the center of attention, you are still answerable for your actions in the court of God. Come the judgment day, God shall ask you about the use of your influence.

The verse also points out that the acknowledgment from someone who is not a family member or a close friend can often hold more significance. Our accomplishments are truly noteworthy and deserving of recognition when we receive praise from a stranger as they have nothing to gain from our adoration (love and respect.)

In essence, proverb 27:2 motivates us to practice humility and discourages us from seeking validation and attention from others, as well as praise from ourselves. The proverbs tell us to prioritize service to others to the point our actions speak for themselves. We can earn the respect and admiration of those around us, without having to boast or promote ourselves

5

Speech

The word "Speech" is defined as the use of words and letters by humans to convey messages and communicate with each other. The Book of Proverbs emphasizes the power of speech and advice that we use our words carefully and wisely.

The collection relating to speech in the book of Proverbs offers guidance on different aspects of speech, including honesty, kindness, and discretion.

The book also warns against the misuse of words, implying that the carelessness of words can cause division and discord. God declares that speaking deceitfully and spreading gossip is shameful utilization of the tongue given to us by Himself. Still, that topic is saved for later discussion in the chapter. So, all things considered, the book encourages us to seek the counsel of wise and motives the readers to listen more than speak.

A reminder: As we progress with the next few chapters of this book, we have already agreed to the fact that the book of Proverbs is one of the most prominent books in the Bible that provides wisdom for everyday living. It is a collection of practical sayings, teachings, and advice provided by the Lord himself through his various communication channels that are often presented in short and concise explanations. In the book of Proverbs, the power of speech is mentioned repeatedly, and so is the importance of using it wisely.

The book of Proverbs compiled by Solomon highlights the fact that our words have the power to build up or tear down, to heal or to harm, and to encourage or to discourage. Proverbs 10:11, states that "The mouth of the righteous is a fountain of life, but the mouth of the wicked conceals violence." This means that the words of a righteous person bring elation, energy, and enlightenment to those around them. When a righteous person speaks, all those who follow or have a connection with them feel inspired, whereas the words of the wicked only bring contempt and hatefulness because they are filled with deceit and destruction.

People who are wicked commonly speak hastily and carelessly. The book of Proverbs warns us against the dangers of speaking hastily and carelessly in verse, "The one who has knowledge uses words with restraint, and whoever has understanding is eventempered. Even fools are thought wise if they keep silent, and discerning if they hold their tongues."—Proverbs 17:27–28

The verse announces that those who speak wisely and thoughtfully are more likely to be viewed as knowledgeable and discerning, whereas those who speak recklessly (hastily) and without thought are considered foolish. In my understanding, people who speak hastily have no regard for others. They don't care about hurting another human's feelings; therefore, they choose to say whatever comes to their mind.

The significance of honesty and integrity in our communication is also highlighted in the book of Proverbs. Verse 12:22 states that "The Lord detests lying lips, but he delights in people who are trustworthy." This verse encourages us to speak the truth. Lord loves his followers when their speech is truthful and honest and when they refrain from using deceitful speech to gain an advantage over others. So, as the followers of Christ, it is our responsibility to utter truth and bypass the opportunity of misguiding others.

The words that come out of our mouths have the power to bring both blessings and curses upon ourselves. In Proverbs 18:21, the book states that "The tongue has the power of life and death, and those who love it will eat its fruit." This means that the words we speak not only affect those around us but they also have an impact on our own lives and the outcomes we experience. So the next time you choose to say something hurtful to a friend, remember that it can impact your life and relationships in the future.

VERSES TO REVIEW

Proverbs 18:21

The tongue has the power of life and death, and those who love it will eat its fruit.—Proverbs 18:21 (New International Version)

Proverbs 10:19

When there are many words, transgression is unavoidable, but he who restrains his lips is wise.—Proverbs 10:19 (New American Standard Bible)

Proverbs 26:4

Don't respond to the words of a fool with more foolish words, or you will become as foolish as he is!—Proverbs 26:4 (The Passion Translation)

Proverbs 10:32

The lips of the godly speak helpful words, but the mouth of the wicked speaks perverse words.—Proverbs 10:32 (New Living Translation)

Proverbs 15:28

Lovers of God think before they speak, but the careless blurt out wicked words meant to cause harm.—Proverbs 15:28 (The Passion Translation)

Proverbs 26:28

A lying tongue hates its victims, and a flattering mouth works ruin.—Proverbs 26:28 (English Standard Version)

Proverbs 11:13

A gossip betrays a confidence, but a trustworthy person keeps a secret.—Proverbs 11:13 (New International Version)

Proverbs 22:11

He who loves purity of heart, and whose speech is gracious, will have the king as his friend.—Proverbs 22:11 (English Standard Version)

Proverbs 15:1

Respond gently when you are confronted and you'll defuse the rage of another. Responding with sharp, cutting words will only make it worse. Don't you know that being angry can ruin the testimony of even the wisest of men?—Proverbs 15:1 (The Passion Translation)

Proverbs 29:20

Do you see a man who is hasty in his words? There is more hope for a fool than for him.—Proverbs 29:20 (English Standard Version)

Proverbs 13:3

Guard your words and you'll guard your life, but if you don't control your tongue, it will ruin everything.—Proverbs 13:3 (The Passion Translation)

Proverbs 21:23

Those who guard their mouths and their tongues guard themselves from trouble.—Proverbs 21:23 (Common English Bible)

Proverbs 31:26

She opens her mouth with wisdom, and the teaching of kindness is on her tongue.—Proverbs 31:26 (English Standard Version)

Proverbs 12:18

Reckless words are like the thrusts of a sword, cutting remarks meant to stab and to hurt. But the words of the wise soothe and heal.—Proverbs 12:18 (The Passion Translation)

Proverbs 29:11

> Fools vent their anger, but the wise quietly hold it back.—
> Proverbs 29:11 (New Living Translation)

EXPLANATION

Proverbs 26:4 advises against reacting spontaneously or hastily to something that has been said to a person we know or to us. Patience is the virtue of a believer, so we should always practice patience. Similarly, it is important to exercise temperateness and thoughtfulness in our speech rather than allowing our emotions to take over our responses. Overall, this proverb teaches us that our words can have a powerful impact, albeit better or worse. Therefore, it is advised to speak thoughtfully and with intention.

Proverbs 15:1 again emphasizes the power of words and the impact they can have on others. The sentence "Respond gently when you are confronted, and you'll defuse the rage of another. Responding with sharp, cutting words will only make it worse" greatly describes how our words can bear two situations; they can either diffuse or inflate a situation. The choice to diffuse or inflate a situation ultimately rests with us; it's only a matter of choosing our words wisely. God, through this proverb, suggests that the generous and compassionate behavior of an individual will lead to conflict resolution while showing harshness and aggression will most likely escalate the tension. Ultimately, this proverb serves as a reminder to all of us that our words have the power to either build up or tear down, which is exactly why it is important to use our words with wisdom and care.

Proverbs 26:28 points us to the fact that there is a distinction between appreciation and flattery. Appreciation is more organic and is something that comes directly from the heart. Whereas flattery is excessive and insincere praise given to further one's own interest and agenda. So what should we do with either of these? The wise of us will accept appreciation and give it back. Also, the wise will not be imitated by flattery but rather see through it for what it is and not be misled by its deceitful nature. Let it be known that people, in the end, appreciate frankness more than flattery. Open criticism from a caring person is much better than hidden love; wounds from a friend are better than kisses from an enemy! So, we should be thankful to a friend or anyone else in our life who is sincere to us. We need to acknowledge their criticism because it would be thousands of times better than flattery from the unknown.

Proverbs 11:13 conscious us about the troubles of gossip. Gossip is harmful because it births rumors. A trustworthy man will try to quiet the rumors, but a man with ill intentions will sow more arguments. Gossip brings divide among the greatest of friends since idle lips are the devil's mouthpiece. The verse also discourages us from unrequired slander as one of the phrases in the verse states, "To slander is to be a fool."

So after taking the verse into consideration, we shouldn't say anything negative about our neighbors and friends, even if they had been mean to us in the past. Instead of badmouthing them, we should go and discuss the matter with them privately. Bear in mind that fire goes out for the lack of fuel, and tensions disappear when gossip halts. We should use our words to defend those who are helpless or lack the power to defend themselves. Remember that God delights in kind words; good demeanor and conduct bring happiness and delight. Let kindness be the rule for everything you say.

In conclusion, the book of Proverbs provides timeless wisdom on the importance of speech and the power of our words. It reminds us to speak wisely, honestly, and with integrity and to use our words to bring life and blessing to those around us.

6

Leadership

Leadership is an amazing human quality. The book of Proverbs offers great insights into leadership and emphasizes its importance, especially for those who hold the position of authority.

The text in the Book of Proverbs warns against the dangers of leaders who are dishonest, oppressive, egotistic, and cowardly. After explaining the dangers, the book offers sort of a prototype of how leaders should be.

If you ask your parents to read your stories from the Bible, you will notice that a lot of leaders of the bygone days were blessed with all of the natural gifts and qualities of a strong leader, but they lost everything because of their pride. Those leaders thought of themselves as superiors to others, and they thought their existence was more important than the people they ruled. Hence, they ended up worsening their own, as well as others, circumstances. So, what is the learning in all of this? We should maintain a balance between power and our existence as leaders. Often times in a leadership role or position, we will be given power. But not getting carried away with it should be our only priority because otherwise, we would end up as the leaders of bygone years. If history teaches us anything, it is to not repeat the mistakes that were made by our ancestors and historical leaders. Therefore, we should showcase humility in places where we are allotted leadership.

A leader could be anyone; he/she/they could lead or command a group, organization, or country. There are leaders in every social gathering. The person who calls the shots and sets the tempo for music in a musical setting is most definitely the leader of the band. A film director is the leader of a movie production; all the actors, writers, costume designers, and sound technicians look at him or her for directions. Similarly, a president is the leader of a country whose decisions affect the population of a country as a whole. Over the years on this planet Earth, we have seen some great leaders and some not-so-great ones as well. American President Abraham Lincoln and South African President Nelson Mandela fall under the category of great leaders because of their significant contributions to the betterment of their respective nations. Mandela stood firmly against apartheid (a system of discrimination on the bases of different skin color) and even went to prison for it. Abraham Lincoln was widely renowned for his leadership during the Civil War and his efforts to end slavery in the United States.

Meanwhile, people like the German Fuhrer, Adolf Hitler, who carried out the genocide of six million Jews, is commonly seen as negative role models and terrible examples of leader. So what makes someone an impressionable and influential leader? In the book of Proverbs, a leader is described as someone who is humble, honest, and just. It says that true leaders lead by example, and their actions promote trust and respect in others. The book of Proverbs also shows a connection between wisdom and leadership. A leader, when granted wisdom, becomes wise; therefore, the decisions they make have clarity of thought as well as care for others. An impressionable leader will never shy away from seeking knowledge and understanding. They will listen to advice and make an informed decision based on that advice. They will be rational and also mindful of the repercussions of their actions.

Besides wisdom, the Proverbs emphasize the significance of righteousness in leadership. The decisions taken by a righteous leader will generally feature integrity and honesty because their upbringing had taught them to uphold the principles of justice and fairness. The yearning desire to take a bribe for personal gain will not sway them as they are fueled by a sense of morality and a desire to do what is right.

VERSES TO REVIEW

Proverbs 19:20

> Listen well to wise counsel and be willing to learn from correction so that by the end of your life you'll be known for your wisdom.—Proverbs 19:20 (The Passion Translation)

Proverbs 12:1

> To learn the truth you must long to be teachable, or you can despise correction and remain ignorant.—Proverbs 12:1 (The Passion Translation)

Proverbs 28:13

> Whoever conceals his transgressions will not prosper, but he who confesses and forsakes them will obtain mercy.—Proverbs 28:13 (English Standard Version)

Proverbs 4:26–27

> Give careful thought to the paths for your feet and be steadfast in all your ways. Do not turn to the right or the left; keep your foot from evil.—Proverbs 4:26–27 (New International Version)

Proverbs 3:5–6

Trust in the Lord with all your heart, and do not lean on your own understanding. In all your ways acknowledge him, and he will make straight your paths.—Proverbs 3:5–6 (English Standard Version)

Proverbs 4:23

Above all else, guard your heart, for everything you do flows from it.—Proverbs 4:23 (New International Version)

Proverbs 4:18

But the path of the righteous is like the light of dawn, which shines brighter and brighter until full day.—Proverbs 4:18 (English Standard Version)

Proverbs 18:10

The name of the Lord is a strong tower; the righteous man runs into it and is safe.—Proverbs 18:10 (English Standard Version)

Proverbs 16:3

Before you do anything, put your trust totally in God and not in yourself. Then every plan you make will succeed.—Proverbs 16:3 (The Passion Translation)

Proverbs 16:9

Within your heart you can make plans for your future, but the Lord chooses the steps you take to get there.—Proverbs 16:9 (The Passion Translation)

Proverbs 16:17

The road of those who do right turns away from evil; those who protect their path guard their lives.—Proverbs 16:17 (Common English Bible)

Proverbs 19:21

Many are the plans in the mind of a man, but it is the purpose of the Lord that will stand.—Proverbs 19:21 (English Standard Version)

Proverbs 6:10–11

A little sleep, a little slumber, a little folding of the hands to rest, and poverty will come upon you like a robber, and want like an armed man.—Proverbs 6:10–11 (English Standard Version)

Proverbs 1:32–33

"For the turning away of the naive will kill them, and the careless ease of [self-righteous] fools will destroy them. But whoever listens to me (Wisdom) will live securely and in confident trust and will be at ease, without fear or dread of evil."—Proverbs 1:32–33 (Amplified Bible)

Proverbs 29:2

> When the righteous increase, the people rejoice, but
> when the wicked rule, the people groan.—Proverbs 29:2
> (English Standard Version)

EXPLANATION

The verses in Proverbs 12:1 brings up the characteristics that one should have in order to become a leader. "To learn the truth, you must long to be teachable" means that a person who aspires to be a leader should have the willingness to learn and should be open to correction as it would allow them to gain wisdom and knowledge to become leaders. The verse furthermore claims that those who are teachable and accepting of their mistakes are more likely to grow in understanding, while those who refuse to change and learn will most likely remain ignorant.

Proverbs 28:13 highlights the importance of honesty, which is another characteristic of a righteous leader. The use of the word 'transgression' in this verse is quite interesting. By definition, transgression means an offense or an act that goes against a law, rule, or code of conduct. The proverb employs the term 'transgression' to suggest that individuals who conceal or hide their wrongdoing will not lead to success or prosperity but rather lead to guilt, shame, and further transgression. On the flip side, the proverb indicates that the individuals who confess and renounce their transgression will receive mercy and forgiveness from God.

The proverb also brings up the idea that confessing our wrongdoing to God through prayer (Protestant denominations) or through confessionals in the presence of a priest (Roman Catholic tradition) is not enough. The third stage of confession, repentance, is as important as acknowledging your sins and wrongdoings in the first place. We must forsake transgression and avoid repeating the mistakes we made in the past if we are to become the next generation of great leaders like Nelson Mandela, Mahatma Gandhi, and Abraham Lincoln.

Proverbs 4:26–27 is an extremely important consideration for leaders. It urges leaders, as well as common folks, to give careful thought to the paths they choose to take in life and to be resolute in their decisions. There will be times when we, as leaders, will be tempted to branch off from the path of righteousness. In those times, we must remain resolute in our cause. The verse and proverb use 'path' as a metaphor to represent the course of one's life. God being the speaker in this verse, advises us (listeners) to be intentional in choosing our path—this means we should find something that interests us and then stick to it. Finding our area of interest can provide us with a path. It is crucial to remain on that path and avoid any detours or distractions that might lead us astray. Finally, this proverb recommends that as wise leaders, we should remain vigilant against evil and temptation, making sure to protect our feet from any wrongdoings.

Proverbs 6:10–11 is hugely captivating. It firstly warns us against laziness and the consequence that can result from neglecting our (leadership) responsibilities. Even small amounts of laziness, such as little sleep and rest, can ultimately lead to poverty and needfulness.

Why and how, you may ask. The answer is beautifully presented using vivid imagery in this verse. The proverb compares poverty and robbery. It says that poverty is when a robber suddenly appears and steals away one's resources, whereas 'needfulness' or 'want' is when the robber who is armed threatens one's security and livelihood. Overall, the proverb gives a clear message that laziness and neglect can have serious consequences. It says that as leaders and followers of the Holy One, we should always remain proactive in regard to our work and resist the temptation of 'doing nothing' and wasting time. If we remain idle, no one will save us from the consequences of poverty and needfulness, and we will never be able to achieve success and security in life.

Proverbs 1:32–33 speaks of some of the main qualities a leader should possess. The proverb warns against the dangers of being simple and foolish. If someone who is positioned in place of a leader turns away from wisdom and chooses to be complacent and careless, they will ultimately bring destruction onto themselves. The proverb uses strong language to describe the dangers of becoming complacent and careless. Becoming simple is described as "killing them," whereas the complacency of a fool is believed to be "destroying" them. In contrast to that, the verse makes a promise to those who are open to knowledge and understanding. God, through this verse, promises that those who seek wisdom will live in security and in confident trust, and they will not feel afraid of evil.

BONUS VERSE

God has a message for those who believe they are entitled and deserve every promotion:

> Don't demand to be promoted as though you were some powerful prince. It is better to wait for a promotion than to be publically refused and disgraced! Fools will end in shame. But if you promote wisdom, it will promote you. Hold it fast, and it would lead you to great honor. Be wise, be patient, and hardworking. And you will be promoted. You will even stand before kings.
> Proverbs 3:35/ 4:7–9/22:29/ 25:6, 7, 27

7

Money

One of the crucial aspects in a person's life is money. Although having it in sufficient amount is a necessity, the lust of acquiring money can have grave consequences. There are various conundrums in this world that we have limited understanding of. To gain a complete understanding of these mysteries and avoid any disrespect towards God through improper use of them, it may be beneficial to seek guidance from the word of God.

So what does the word of God, i.e., the book of Proverbs say about money?

The book offers significant insights on money and wealth. It demands that we spend our money diligently and approach all our financial matters wisely. The book also highlights the dangers of greed and debt, and it calls for us to remain honest in our pursuit of wealth. The book also advises us to remain content with what our Lord has given to us. In a commanding manner God conveys through his Proverbs that we should show generosity towards those with financial complications.

The book of Proverbs makes a comparison between inheritance and wealth, both of which are forms of money. It is mentioned that when a goqd man dies, he leaves behind inheritance to his children or grandchildren. However, when a sinister dies, his wealth is stored up for the godly, meaning that all the money he has gather is rendered useless as soon as he dies. The sinister cannot take his money to his grave or buy angels in heaven. He cannot use the money he has run after his entire life to secure a transfer to heaven from hell.

The book of proverb states that a father can give his children homes and riches, but the best inheritance is godliness. This also means that it is a privilege to have honest parents.

The book of proverb encourages us, the loyal followers of Jesus Christ and believers of God's existence to save diligently and spend only when required. The book says that a wise man would save for his future, meanwhile the foolish man will spend whatever he gets. The wise person will also save money by being on the lookout for bargains, as they know that there is nothing wrong with bargaining. Whether by bargaining or resisting urges, a sensible person saves money and grows their wealth. Although saving is a welcomed choice and a great initiative, the book of proverb also highlights the consequence of holding money too tight. When we hold on to our wealth too tightly, it is possible that we will lose everything. Therefore, it is important to give away and become richer.

Under the subject of money, the book of proverb expresses God's disapproval towards those who withhold repayment of debts. God, through Proverbs governs us against delaying payment when we have money. The book of Proverbs dissuades us from saying to our lenders, "some other time," if we are accomplished to repayment. In the context of debt, the book concludes with a reminder: "Just as the rich rule the poor, similarly the borrower is servant to the lender."

Being rich or having more money than other isn't necessarily a bad thing. In fact, God encourages us to make money and gives an indication of the person who would make profit. King Solomon, inspired by God writes, "Any enterprise built by wise planning, becomes strong through common sense, and profits wonderfully by keeping abreast of the facts."

Solomon further writes on the subject of profit and gain: "A little gained honestly is better than great wealth gotten by dishonest means." King Solomon then gives an example of men who generate wealth and buy things with dishonest means. He says that those men would enjoy cheating for a while but the moment they buy something (a cake) with ill-gotten gain (profit) the cake would turn to gravel in their mouths. Not only the gain gravel their mouths, it would impact the whole family, bringing grief. Solomon, inspired by God's word in the bible says that Quick Wealth is not a blessing in the end. This begs that question; when dishonest gain never lasts, what is the point of taking the risk?

"Work brings profit, but talk brings poverty!" **Proverbs 9:11 / 14:23/ 15:31, 32**

Something noble as charity is associated with money. This is why you will find so many proverbs on "Giving." The book of Proverb suggests that the creation of Lord should honor him by giving him the first part of their income. In return God will cause everything they do to multiply and guarantee success. The cause of righteousness is advanced by the good man's earning, and the sinful man will waste his earnings on his sins. So how one could honor God and give him the first part of income? The answer is charity. When we give to the poor we are basically lending our income to the Lord. Rest assured, God gives great interest on the money we lend him. This is exactly how we could give away and still be richer in the future. In the context of charity, it is important to keep in mind that the generous man shall always be rich. By watering others, he waters himself.

The Almighty that resides in the skies know everything. He knew that his beloved creations would introduce payment methods, a barter of exchange to exchange goods and services. He also knew that his creations would fall into traps, deceived by the conniving. So he provided us with guidance for investing our money wisely.

In the book of Proverbs, God directs us to steer clear of investment schemes that claim to make a person rich instantly. God says that those schemes are evil and lead to poverty. Then, he instructs us to inspect our investment before committing ourselves. It is crucial to know all the facts and make sure to examine the past record of the investment. In the continuation of proverb that guides us about investing our money, God illustrates with an example of how diminishing it is to put confidence in something that is unreliable. God through the proverb conveys, "For putting confidence in something unreliable is like chewing with a sore tooth."

VERSES TO REVIEW

Proverbs 10:4

> Lazy hands make for poverty, but diligent hands bring wealth.—Proverbs 10:4 (New International Version)

Proverbs 12:23

> A prudent man conceals knowledge, but the heart of fools proclaims folly.—Proverbs 12:23 (English Standard Version)

Proverbs 21:20

> The wise have wealth and luxury, but fools spend whatever they get.—Proverbs 21:20 (New Living Translation)

Proverbs 11:24

> One gives freely, yet grows all the richer; another withholds what he should give, and only suffers want.—Proverbs 11:24 (English Standard Version)

Proverbs 14:15

The simple believes everything, but the prudent gives thought to his steps.—Proverbs 14:15 (English Standard Version)

Proverbs 11:15

Whoever puts up security for a stranger will surely suffer, but whoever refuses to shake hands in pledge is safe.—Proverbs 11:15 (New International Version)

Proverbs 12:11

Work hard at your job and you'll have what you need. Following a get-rich-quick scheme is nothing but a fantasy.—Proverbs 12:11 (The Passion Translation)

Proverbs 21:17

Whoever loves pleasure will be a poor man; he who loves wine and oil will not be rich.—Proverbs 21:17 (English Standard Version)

Proverbs 3:9

Glorify God with all your wealth, honoring him with your very best, with every increase that comes to you.—Proverbs 3:9 (The Passion Translation)

Proverbs 28:22

> Greedy people try to get rich quick but don't realize they're headed for poverty.—Proverbs 28:22 (New Living Translation)

Proverbs 22:7

> The rich rules over the poor, and the borrower is the slave of the lender.—Proverbs 22:7 (English Standard Version)

EXPLANATION

Proverbs 12:23 contrasts the behavior of a wise person with that of a foolish person. The first half of the verse calls wise person a "prudent man," and claims that a wise person will choose to keep certain knowledge or information to themselves rather than sharing it openly. He would do so because he rightly believes that not all information should be shared publically. He knows that God has specifically created somethings to remain a secret until the judgment days. In modern day example, you would know that people are discouraged to go into deep waters or places like the Bermuda Triangle.

The second half of the proverb speaks of the individual that is completely opposite of the prudent man. The verse refer to him as "fool," and suggests that such people are more likely to share everything they know, even if it is foolish or unwise. The phrase "the heart of fools proclaims folly" suggests that foolish people are more concerned with showing off their knowledge. They are the attention seekers of the society and they are more concerned with being heard rather than being answerable to appropriateness of what they are saying.

Proverbs 11:15 warns us about the potential dangers of money transactions with strangers. The verse's first half warns us that if we put up some of our valuable item as collateral or acts as a guarantor for a stranger, we will likely suffer negative consequences in the form of theft or fraud. When we act as a guarantor for a stranger, we are taking on a significant financial risk without knowing the person well or having any assurance that they will honor their end of the deal.

The second half of the verse offers exhibits a different scenario, one where a person refuses to make such pledges or guarantees. That person is certainly safer because they are not taking any risk with a stranger. Ultimately, that person has avoided the uncertainties associated with doing business with a stranger.

Overall, this proverb emphasizes the importance of caution and discernment when it comes to spending currency in the form of investment, especially with people who are not well-known or trusted. This proverb suggests that avoiding such transactions altogether may be the safest approach to safeguarding their money.

8

Relationships

Regarding relationships, the book requests us to be kind, honest, caring in our interactions with each and other. It tells us to form relationships free from dishonesty, arrogance, and anger. "Lying lips are an abomination to the lord, but those who act faithfully are his delight."

The book calls for understanding the two types of relationships. One is characterized by romance, while the other pertains to connections we form with ordinary people in our society like us. We don't have a romantic attraction to other people, but it doesn't mean that we treat them any less than the people we love. The book of Proverbs calls for understanding that we must act differently in each of our relationships but not lose our personality. By doing so, we can cultivate meaningful and fulfilling connections with others that bring joy and enrichment to our lives.

If you flip back pages and return to chapter three of this book, you will see that I have written about how God commands us to be like Locusts as they have no King, but they still march in formation. That same example could be applied here as well. There is a lot to learn from the tiny insect known as Locust. Although the tiny insect doesn't have a dialect, observing the conduct of the life of a Locust can teach us valuable lessons on how we, as humans, should approach and conduct our living. Among the four things that are small and listed in the book of Proverbs, Locusts are considered wise because they stay together in the swarms, even though they don't have a leader. We humans, too, live in swarms; however, we have named them communities. Our communities consist of our families, friends, and neighbors. Residing within communities naturally fosters a sense of affection and affinity towards fellowship, and since we strongly value fellowship, those of us who are wicked will typically find wicked companions, while those of us generous and godly will automatically foster relationships with the godly companions. The book of Proverbs tells the godly among us to celebrate because the godly citizen brings good influence with themselves, which causes a community to prosper. Whereas it suggests that the wicket drives the community to its downfall because the wicked is synonymous with moral decay.

God, through his wisdom in the book of Proverbs, implies that kindness is the only way to create meaningful relationships. He mentions that a believer should never get tired of being kind. Displaying kindness towards fellow beings shows the noble-mindedness of a believer. God, using his dialect in the book of Proverbs, commands us to hold on to the virtue of kindness and to kindness our motivation because it makes a person more attractive. It would be beneficial for us if we let kindness be the rule for everything we say and do. God even goes far ahead to say that our souls are nurtured when we demonstrate any kind of kindness, while they are weakened and destroyed when we are cruel.

RELATIONSHIP WITH NEIGHBORS

Our Lord dwelling in the heavens abode encourages us to be a great neighbors. He instructs us to demonstrate great companionship skills to our neighbors and to always be helpful whenever needed.

Neighbors should trust each other and look after each other's interests. The trust neighbors have between them is built overtime and not just in one single night. It is of utmost importance to value and maintain the trust we have with one another, ensuring that we refrain from speaking against each other, acting in ways that betray that trust, or plotting against our neighbors. We can only strive to build the aforementioned trust when we stop perceiving them as ordinary people that we encounter on a daily basis. In truth, they are much more than just the people who live around you and the people you happen to like. With that being said, bear in mind not to visit your neighbors too often because there is a chance that you will outwear your welcome.

PROVERBS TO REVIEW

A man of many companions may come to ruin, but there is a friend who sticks closer than a brother.—Proverbs 18:24 (English Standard Version)

The eye that mocks a father and scorns to obey a mother will be picked out by the ravens of the valley and eaten by the vultures.—Proverbs 30:17 (English Standard Version)

Like one who takes away a garment in cold weather, and like vinegar on soda, is one who sings songs to a heavy heart.—Proverbs 25:20 (New King James Version)

If you want to grow in wisdom, then spend time with the wise. Walk with the wicked, and you'll eventually become just like them.—Proverbs 13:20 (The Passion Translation)

Drive out a scoffer, and strife will go out, and quarreling and abuse will cease.—Proverbs 22:10 (English Standard Version)

A friend loves at all times, and a brother is born for adversity.—Proverbs 17:17 (English Standard Version)

A brother who has been insulted is harder to win back than a walled city, and arguments separate people like the barred gates of a palace.—Proverbs 18:19 (New Century Version)

With patience, a ruler may be persuaded, and a soft tongue will break a bone.—Proverbs 25:15 (English Standard Version)

A scoffer does not like to be reproved; he will not go to the wise.—Proverbs 15:12 (English Standard Version)

A peaceful heart leads to a healthy body; jealousy is like cancer in the bones.—Proverbs 14:30 (New Living Translation)

Iron sharpens iron, and one man sharpens another.—Proverbs 27:17 (English Standard Version)

EXPLANATION

This verse **18:24** from the book of Proverbs highlights the importance of having a true and faithful friend. In His efforts to facilitate our comprehension, God presents two contrasting ideas about relationships. The first part describes a person who has many companions and superficial friendships. In that same part, it is suggested that such a person may eventually suffer abandoning or downfall. The message here is that we can rely on a large network of acquaintances, but without deep connections, our superficial friend circle may not provide support in the time of need and be loyal to us.

In the second contrasting idea about relationships, God, in the book of Proverbs, emphasizes the value of a genuine friend who remains loyal and resolute. God designates this friend as someone more worthy than a brother, signifying a bond that is even stronger and more dependable than that of siblings. If we are fortunate enough to find ourselves in this type of friendship, we can rejoice knowing that we have someone we can trust, seek support from, and rely on for unwavering companionship. A genuine friend who remains loyal and resolute is vehemently a great source of comfort, encouragement, and assistance in times of need.

From an overall perspective, Proverbs 18:24 encourages us to cultivate and cherish meaningful friendships, emphasizing the benefits of having a trustworthy and loyal companion who stands by our side through thick and thin. It encourages us to think of friendship less as a commodity and more as a tremendous blessing and a source of stability in our life.

The proverb 30:17 presents a strong warning about the consequences of disrespecting and dishonoring one's parents. It uses harsh words to present a graphic image to convey the severity of the punishment that awaits those who show contempt towards their parents.

The starting verse says, "The eye that mocks a father." This verse is basically referring to someone who looks down upon, belittles, and disrespects his or her father in metaphorical terms. The person in the example shows a lack of honor and reverence for their father's authority. Then, the phrase says, "Scorns to obey a mother." In this phrase, God is referring to those individuals who reject and disregard their mother's commands or guidance.

After surfacing the illustration of the person who disrespects their parents, the proverb goes on to describe the fate of such a person. The last part of the proverb state that their eye will be "picked out by the ravens of the valley" and "eaten by the vultures." This is where God paints a gruesome and graphic image in front of our eyes using metaphors. The reason for painting such a daunting image is to symbolize a complete and utter downfall or destruction, where the person who dishonors their parents will face a terrible fate.

In a broader sense of the Proverb, God has painted gruesome imagery to remind us all about the importance of honoring and obeying one's parents. The verse, albeit evoking a sense of fear, encourages us to show respect, gratitude, and obedience towards those who have brought us into the world and raised us. As the followers of Jesus Christ and believers of God's authority over the skies above, we must keep in mind that Disregarding or mocking our parent's authority can have severe consequences, not only in the context of the immediate family but also in the overall order and harmony of society.

Proverb 25:15 highlights the importance of patience in forming relationships. The first part of Proverb 25:15 suggests that patience is an indispensable human characteristic when it comes to interacting with rulers or those in powerful positions. The proverb gives us another way to reach out can connect with the people in power. It suggests that instead of resorting to force, aggression, or impatience, we should approach powerful people with patience and tactic, as that can lead us to a more favorable outcome. By exercising restraint and showcasing our calmness and patience in presenting our arguments or concerns, there is a greater chance of persuading or influencing the ruler's decision.

The latter part of the proverb utilizes a metaphor to convey the power of a soft or gentle approach. It declares that a soft tongue will "break a bone," meaning that a gentle, kind, and respectful speech can influence those in dictatorship positions as the patience of man is highly influential and can achieve what force or aggression cannot. Just as a gentle touch can fracture or break a solid bone, a gentle and well-chosen word can have a profound impact, breaking down barriers, resolving conflicts, and winning the hearts of arch enemies.

9

Marriage

Now I know that most of you reading this book are kids. You wake up, get dressed, eat your breakfast, and then go to school. On the weekends and vacations, you earnestly plead with your parents to take you to your grandparent's house. You little angels are seen as innocent being, untouched by the responsibilities of adult life. Unlike adults, your life revolves around simpler joys like spending time with your friends and playing video games in each other's company. Your carefree days may seem far removed from finding a life partner and entering into a lifelong commitment, but that doesn't mean you shouldn't be well prepared for something that will definitely come in your future. As a devoted Christian and concerned motherly figure, I feel that it is my responsibility to introduce you to the idea of choosing a compatible partner while you are still very young. Having this information early on in your life may greatly influence your future happiness and your well-being.

Firstly, I want you to understand marriage. While it is true that you may not grasp the full understanding of this concept without a certain level of emotional maturity and life experience, even if you could only grasp its fundamental aspects, my goal would still be accomplished. In essence, marriage is the coming together of two people in front of the Lord. The two people stand before God and dedicate their lives to each other under the guidance of God.

The fundamentals of marriage will help you identify the qualities of an ideal future partner (Wife or Husband). It will provide you with guidance on what to look for in your future husband or wife, and the philosophy of marriage, coupled with the religious illumination, will empower you to make informed decisions when the time comes. One valuable source of wisdom that contains insightful content on the subject of marriage is the Book of Proverbs.

The Book of Proverbs overflows with philosophical texts, offering a wealth of timeless wisdom and practical advice related to marriage. When I embarked on my spiritual journey and began reading the Book of Proverbs, I immediately recognized that its teachings could be molded to help teach children about the qualities they should look for in a future partner. Rather than presenting marriage as an alien concept, the approach the Book of Proverbs takes is by blending wisdom with easy to understand valuable lessons into the children's moral and ethical education.

The Book says that we should value qualities such as kindness, integrity, wisdom, and respect for others. Subsequently, when choosing a partner, we should judge our partner based on these exact qualities. Choosing a partner based on how they respond to these attributes will not only contribute to a successful relationship, but it will also help foster a harmonious society. The reason I am motivated to familiarize you all with these qualities from an early age is to sow the seeds of understanding, encourage personal growth, and enhance your judgment.

Children can be taught to recognize kindness in others—those who are compassionate, considerate, and empathetic. They can be encouraged to appreciate the importance of integrity and honesty, seeking partners who are trustworthy and who hold themselves to high moral standards. Wisdom, which encompasses good judgment, self-control, and emotional intelligence, can be emphasized as a desirable quality in a potential partner. And respect, both for themselves and for others, should be instilled as a fundamental principle.

The proverbs I have chosen for this chapter are mostly easy to understand. By simply reading those proverbs out, you will gradually internalize these values over time. This means that you will be able to apply the relevance of these qualities in your own lives, utilizing your young minds.

As you grow older and become more mature, the lessons about marriage and the significance of choosing the right partner will continue to guide you, serving as a moral compass in your search for a life partner. As you read these proverbs, you will gain an understanding of what to look for in a potential wife or husband. This will enable you to navigate your future relationships with better judgment and seek partners who embody the qualities you have come to value.

Our Lord tells us through the Book of Proverbs that a father can give his children homes and riches, but only the Lord can give his children understanding mates. Having a mate that understands you is a blessing from God, so we must trust him to bring us the right mate at the right time. The creator of this universe says that a good mate is a joy, but a mate that is mischievous can be the reason for the trouble and decreased strength. That partner will tear down anything we create. A good mate is more than precious gems, so we must trust them as they will richly satisfy our needs. That partner will not hinder us in any way possible. Instead, they will help us for life. In the Book of Proverbs, God cautions us about the troubles of charm. God informs us charm can be deceptive, and beauty doesn't last. Therefore, a partner who fears and reverences God shall be chosen over the person who is obsessed with their flesh.

VERSES TO REVIEW

Proverbs 31:30

> Charm is deceitful, and beauty is vain, but a woman who fears the Lord is to be praised.—Proverbs 31:30 (English Standard Version)

Proverbs 21:19

It's better to live in a hut in the wilderness than with a crabby, scolding spouse!—Proverbs 21:19 (The Passion Translation)

Proverbs 12:4

An excellent wife is the crown of her husband, but she who brings shame is like rottenness in his bones.—Proverbs 12:4 (English Standard Version)

Proverbs 11:16

A gracious woman gains respect, but ruthless men gain only wealth.—Proverbs 11:16 (New Living Translation)

Proverbs 18:22

He who finds a wife finds a good thing and obtains favor from the Lord.—Proverbs 18:22 (English Standard Version)

Proverbs 15:17

It's much better to have a kind, loving family, even with little, than to have great wealth with nothing but hatred and strife all around you.—Proverbs 15:17 (The Passion Translation)

Proverbs 10:22

When the Lord blesses you with riches, you have nothing to regret.—Proverbs 10:22 (Contemporary English Version)

Proverbs 22:6

Start children off on the way they should go, and even when they are old they will not turn from it.—Proverbs 22:6 (New International Version)

Proverbs 31:10

An excellent wife who can find? She is far more precious than jewels.—Proverbs 31:10 (English Standard Version)

EXPLANATION

Proverbs 21:19 highlights the idea that a man could prefer to live in a hut in the wilderness rather than staying a constantly nagging relationship with a spouse. The proverb suggests that constant conflict and nagging from either gender can have a negative impact on one's quality of life. It can even take a toll on a spouse's well-being.

This verse reminds those who are in a relationship about the importance of maintaining harmony and peace within their marriage. As children, you must know that the constant presence of quarrels and bickering between relationships can cause extreme stress and an overwhelming feeling, leading to poor life standards and reduced contentment.

Verse 22:6 (Proverb—New International Version) offers guidance to parents on raising their children. The proverb advises parents or guardians to train their children on the right path from the beginning. This verse also explains why I choose the topic of marriage for this chapter.

This verse implies that the teachings and values bestowed to children in their young years will have a lasting impact on their character and behavior throughout their lives. Let it be known that you will have kids of your own one day. So, as the God's Devotees and the followers of his son, Jesus, it will be your responsibility to establish a strong foundation of faith in your children. Talk to them about marriage and its benefits from a young age. Do not force your belief onto them but bring up the topic of marriage and soulmate while keeping the conversation friendly and healthy. The more well informed your kid is or will be, the better life choice they will make.

The verse in Proverbs 18:22 (English Standard Version) describes finding a spouse as a highly beneficial event in a person's life, particularly for men. The verse conveys that finding a wife is not just a matter of chance or personal preference; in God's viewpoint, it is one of the most remarkable things a man can do to please Him. God favors those who have the rightful intention of finding a wife.

In the context of the Book of Proverbs, this verse highlights the importance of having healthy, loving, and committed relationships. There is a different sort of contentment that a human feels in their life when their marriage is healthy, and the couple is committed and affectionate towards each other. Mondays stop mundaneing as you look forward to seeing your wife at the end of your work shift. The northern lights appear less magical than the aura your wife radiates. All in all, when you choose the right partner and give them your honesty, affection, and care, the positive impact of a harmonious union on an individual's life is immeasurable.

10

Women

Lord gives equal importance to women as He does with men. In His sight and judgment, both the genders are equals and no one is given the endorsement to claim superiority on others.

In the Book of Proverbs, He claims that men and women are both responsible for building a pious home. Both are responsible for raising humble and behaved kids and responsible for creating an environment in the house that supports enlightenment and welcomes the praising of our Lord and his son Jesus.

A virtuous and honorable wife will bring honor and joy to her husband, while a malicious and spiteful wife will bring unpleasantry and quarrels to her husband. A wise and a prudent wife is a blessing and a gift from God. She is valuable without beyond material possessions. It means that those who have wives of bad intentions, must have done others wrong. There is no other explanation why the Lord have given them vindictive partners other than as karma of their bad actions. The woman and wife who embodies gracefulness not only raises her stature as a woman but also elevates her husband's prestige in the society; she is esteemed and immensely respected in society.

There are four things listed in the book of Proverb that are important for us to understand. One of those four things is "the growth of love between a man and a woman." We the wandering human run around directionless in the search of perfect love. We think that our life will be meaningless if we cannot find the perfect partner. The thing is there is no need for man to find a woman or for woman to find a man. All we need to do is have a little faith. Lord says to us that we should listen to his wisdom; if we have dedicated our life and ourselves to the Lord, then he has a perfect time for that 'Partner' to enter our lives. Lord discourages us from spending all our time dating and looking for sweethearts. God wants us to remain unattached and uncommitted because He wants us to figure ourselves out. Only when we know who we are from the inside and the out, then we are ready to share our live with someone. So, don't be disheartened when you cannot find yourself a partner to spend your time with, Lord has everything planned for you! Just have some faith.

An understanding husband or an understanding wife is from the Lord. So if you wait for God's match, your marriage will be worth more than precious gems.

Although choosing the husband or the wife is a personal choice, one shouldn't discount their parent's advice in proposing their partner. The counsel our parents provide is invaluable. They tend to speak from experience; therefore, their opinions should be vigilantly listened and actively practised. Lord asks us to obey our father and mother, take their advice straight to heart, and keep in mind everything they tell us. Lord says that our parent's counselling will lead us to prosperity and save us from harm. Only a fool despises his/her parents' advice. In the Book of Proverb, God emphasizes listening to father's advice and disdains the action of despising the mother's experience. Therefore, similar to all matters regarding life, we should actively seek our parent's advice in proclaiming our partner for life.

VERSES TO REVIEW

Proverbs 31:30

Charm is deceitful, and beauty is vain, but a woman who fears the Lord is to be praised.—Proverbs 31:30 (English Standard Version)

Proverbs 31:31

Honor her for all that her hands have done, and let her works bring her praise at the city gate.—Proverbs 31:31 (New International Version)

Proverbs 31:10

An excellent wife who can find? She is far more precious than jewels.—Proverbs 31:10 (English Standard Version)

Proverbs 11:16

A gracious woman gains respect, but ruthless men gain only wealth.—Proverbs 11:16 (New Living Translation)

Proverbs 31:11

The heart of her husband trusts in her, and he will have no lack of gain.—Proverbs 31:11 (English Standard Version)

Proverbs 27:15

> An endless drip, drip, drip, from a leaky faucet and the
> words of a cranky, nagging wife have the same effect.—
> Proverbs 27:15 (The Passion Translation)

Proverbs 14:1

> Every wise woman encourages and builds up her family,
> but a foolish woman over time will tear it down by her
> own actions.—Proverbs 14:1 (The Passion Translation)

EXPLANATION

The **verse 31:31** is related to the conversation between King Lemuel and his mother. Through this verse, it is understood that King
Lemuel's mother is providing him advice and wisdom about finding a worthy wife. In the wider context, this verse could be used
to teach husband and the Christian community on the subject of
honoring and appreciating virtuous woman for her hardwork and
accomplishments. The phrase "All that her hands have done" calls
attention to the tasks and responsibilities she has fulfilled with
diligence and skill.

By mentioning "the city gate" God, through King Solomon,
informs us that appreciating woman and everything "her hands
have done" is significant. The very mention of the city gate emphasizes the significance of praising wives, as in ancient times, the city
gate was a central gathering place for important discussions and
decision-making.

The **verse 31:10** starts with posing an interesting question:
"An excellent wife, who can find?" the question tells us finding a
truly exceptional wife is a rare, and therefore, a valuable occur-
rence. The verse suggests that only a handful of women possess
the qualities of a noble woman. There is a scarcity of such women.

The second part of the verse says, "She is far more precious than Jewels." In the second part, God puts immense worth and value on a wife that is virtuous. He compares the virtuous wife to something as valuable as jewel. Jewels are highly prized in any commodities market. They are rare, shiny, and pleasing to eyes. In God's judgment a virtuous wife is more precious than jewel, meaning she is more beautiful, valuable, and rarer than anything in this world.

Proverb 14:1 makes a comparison between the actions and outcomes of two different types of women: the wise woman and the foolish woman. The verse uses metaphorical language to demonstrate the outcomes of their behaviors and impact on their households.

The first woman is referred to as "wise" because she builds her home. She deliberately undertakes wise actions to nurture her home which includes her husband and her children. She invests time, effort, and wisdom into building a strong foundation of her house and fosters a positive and healthy environment for her family.

In contrast to that, God gives us an example of a foolish woman. In the verse, God describes that the foolish woman will tear down her house with her own hands, and along with it, the house's peace. Due to her foolishness, she will engage in destructive behavior that would harm her household including her immediate and extended family. Her actions may lead to strained relationships, deterioration of house environment, and finally, the loss of stability and security.

Proverb 27:15 uses vivid imagery to illustrate the negative effects of living with a wife that loves to quarrel and argue. The verse compares her presence to the consistent sound of water dripping during a rainy day, which can be extremely irritating and bothersome.

The never ending quarrels can be disruptive and of frustrating nature. The arguments within a marriage or household benefits neither the man or the woman of the house. It only invites negativity and frustration. Just as the sound of dripping water can get on someone's nerve, creating a sense of unease, the ongoing conflicts caused by a quarrelsome wife can disturb the peace and sanctity of the house. This proverb serves as a reminder of the importance of cultivating a peaceful and harmonious atmosphere within relationships. It highlights the hurtful impact of constant conflict and encourages couples, particularly wives, to put on a gentle and understanding demeanor that fosters unity and peace rather than discord.

Proverbs 31:11, in parts, describes the virtuous woman or wife of noble character. It highlights the relationship between the wife and her husband, specifically focusing on the trust and confidence a husband should have in his wife.

The phrase "The heart of her husband trusts in her" suggests that the husband has complete trust and confidence in his wife. He relies on her and has faith in her character, abilities, and judgment. This trust is essential for a healthy and strong marital relationship.

The second part of the verse states, "and he will have no lack of gain." This part of the verse indicates that a husband who trusts his wife will experience benefits and prosperity. Through this proverb, God is trying to communicate that a woman of trustworthy nature, wisdom, and efforts will most likely contribute to the overall success and prosperity of the family. Her well intended actions and decisions will positively translate into the household income as well as the overall well-being of the family.

www.ingramcontent.com/pod-product-compliance
Lightning Source LLC
Chambersburg PA
CBHW050015090426
42734CB00020B/3273